THE
SCHOOL
FOR *Wives*

Molière
L'École des femmes

A Translation in Rhymed Verse

Maria-Cristina Necula

To order additional copies of this book, contact:
Xlibris Corporation
1-888-795-4274
www.Xlibris.com
Orders@Xlibris.com
68196

PREFACE

Translating any text is a very challenging experience. One must try to stay as close to the original as possible, yet a completely literal translation is not always a good one. Being faithful to the original constitutes only one aspect of translating. Since it is impossible to obtain a perfectly accurate translation, each translator must endeavor to render the "flavor" of the original text in the best way possible. In order to do that, one has to take into account not only the language of translation with its idioms and expressions that would best fit the spirit of the original, but also the time period in which the translation is completed and the culture of the language in which the text is being translated. In other words, if a text would be translated in English in the beginning of the century, and then, translated again in the present, the two versions of translation would be different as each translator would use the idiomatic expressions understandable to his/her contemporaries. I assume that there would also be a difference between an English translation by a British translator (geared towards British readers) and one by an American translator (for American readers). Even though both societies employ the same language, the everyday idiomatic flavor of speech with its expressions is different from one culture to the other. This is particularly important to keep in mind when translating Molière who, in all of his plays, uses allusions and expressions meaningful to his contemporary audience. His colloquialisms should be rendered by colloquialisms that speak to the translator's contemporaries.

If translating a text in prose is challenging, translating a play in rhymed verse is doubly so. All of a sudden, staying close to the text and rendering its flavor are not enough anymore for the translator has become subject to the tyranny of the two "gods" of rhyme and rhythm. These two demand equal respect and attention, and are always in competition with the other translation tyrant: faithfulness to the text. Countless times I found myself wondering which is more important. For the most part, I was forced to find a compromise between these three elements; the rhyme seemed to be most demanding of all. True, I could have translated *L'école des femmes* into blank verse, but I felt that this would have betrayed the author more than the act of taking a few liberties or making several inversions required by the rhyme (and rhythm). Not to mention the fact that the spirit of Molière's plays is found not only in the meaning of the words and sentences, but also in the sound and rhythm of what is being said. The twelve-syllable verse and rhymed couplet (Alexandrine)instantly transport one back in time and make the translation more faithful to Molière.

There are a few liberties which I've taken regarding expressions. For example, in Act I, Arnolphe tells Chrysalde why he will avoid marrying a clever woman:

"And I know what it costs some men to have married

Smart women. Now they wish they were dead and buried."

and later:

"No. I refuse to wed a complicated brain.

A woman who can write is a guaranteed pain!"

Obviously, the American expressions of being "dead and buried" and someone being "a pain" are nowhere to be found in Molière's play. Aside from the fact that they provided rhymes for "married" and "brain" respectively, these idioms helped me to express a certain arrogant sarcasm characteristic of Arnolphe. These expressions show, first of all, his condescending pity towards those men who married smart women. According to him, the horror of it is so immense that they'd rather be dead. But that is not going to happen to him (that's what he thinks!) so he dismisses clever women by saying they are a pain, not even worth bothering with.

Another inevitable aspect of translating a play in rhymed verse is the need to use grammatical inversions. Molière himself uses them. Sometimes he is forced to by the exigencies of the rhyme, but other times he employs them for variety. For the most part, I used them because the rhyme required it. An example is in Act II when Arnolphe curses the old woman who had visited Agnes:

"Ah! poisoner of hearts! Damned witch, may you be cursed!

For your kind acts, by hell may you be reimbursed!"

Another is in Act V when Arnolphe confronts Agnes:

"Yes, you! . . . who can set up a nightly rendezvous

And run out secretly, your lover to pursue."

In standard grammatical order, the second verse of each couplet would appear as follows:

"May you be reimbursed by hell for your kind acts!"

and:

"And run out secretly to pursue your lover."

In each case, the pressing need for rhyme required an inversion.

A very interesting issue came up when I had to find a way to translate the new title of nobility that Arnolphe gives himself: Monsieur de la Souche. I could have left it exactly as it is. However, in French, "souche" means "stump" or "stem" literally, and figuratively, it means "blockhead". To the French audience and readers, the fact that Arnolphe changes his name to this "noble" title is not only funny, but also revealing of his personality. It is just like him to be so arrogant as to not even realize that his title of nobility links him to an "old tree-stump" or a "blockhead". Here, Molière with his characteristic flair for ridiculing the vain makes Arnolphe pay for his arrogance by giving him a name which says just what he is, and by having him actually liking this name. I felt it would be a loss to the readers if I couldn't find a translation that would transmit that in English. "Blockhead" was a bit too much, so I used the literal meaning of "souche", namely "stump". Thus, Arnolphe ended up calling himself "Sir de Stump". This gave me the opportunity later on to pun on his name as Molière does when he has

Horace unwittingly tell Arnolphe of the "old fool" who keeps his Agnes trapped. In French, Horace says the fool's name is "de la Source" ("of the spring") which is a misunderstanding of "de la Souche". Having used "de Stump", I was able to render Horace's blunder in a more meaningful and, hopefully, funny way to the English-speaking readers. Thus, in English, Arnolphe's name as understood by Horace becomes "de Clump" or "de Plump".

Sometimes I had a lot of trouble with the way one sentence was spread or structured within a couplet. At times, a sentence would fit perfectly in one verse. In other instances, a sentence would begin in the middle or at the end of one verse and end in the middle of the next verse. There were countless variations. I found that here and there I was forced to break up a sentence between verses in awkward places. An example of that is in Act V when Horace meets Arnolphe:

"Horace: Sir Arnolphe?

Arnolphe: Yes. But you? . . .

Horace: It's Horace. I was just

                On my way to ask you for a favor. You must

                Get up pretty early!"

The sentence "You must get up pretty early!" is divided at an unusual place (after "must") for the sake of the rhyme. I tried to avoid such unusual break-ups of sentences and I did for the most part, but sometimes they are inevitable.

I also had to deal with an issue that I had not expected at first, but that did present some problems: the issue of length. For example, it happened several times that the translation came out shorter in length than the French original. Thus, I would take a couplet (two verses) which expressed an idea in French, and find that this same idea only took me a verse and a half to express in English. So I was left with an unused half a verse. The way I solved this problem was to use repetition. For instance, in Act V, Arnolphe says:

"Le jour se va paraître et je vais consulter

Comment dans ce malheur je me dois comporter."

My translation was:

"It's dawn. I must think of how to behave in the face

Of such a misfortune, what to do in this case."

If the translation would have ended at the word "misfortune", it would have rendered precisely what Molière had written. However, since this couplet came out half a verse short in English, I needed to "fill-up" the remaining half-verse, keeping in mind the rhyme. Therefore, I emphasized the author's idea by repeating what he has said, but with different words. Thus Arnolphe has to think not only of "how to behave in the face of such a misfortune," but also "what to do in this case" (the case of misfortune). This "unequal length" issue, challenged me to take some liberties and add words that were not in the original. I strived to keep those added words faithful to the character's original words by using repetition, emphasis and sometimes logical deduction from what the character was saying. Another example is right at the beginning of the play:

"Chrysalde: So you say you've returned to ask her for her hand?

Arnolphe: I want to get it done by morning, as I planned."

The words "as I planned" are my own. To be completely faithful to Molière would mean to end my translation after "morning." However, I needed three more words to complete the verse and make it rhyme with "hand." "As I planned" is a way for Arnolphe to emphasize that the act of asking for Agnes' hand has been well thought out and planned. As a matter of fact, later on we find out that it has been planned since Agnes was four years old. The "logical deduction" approach shows that since he is going to ask her, he must have planned it before. Thus, those three extra words serve to put in writing what can be deduced from "between the lines."

I found that translation requires a variety of skills which, when taken separately, can actually contradict each other. On one hand, one needs to have the intellectual flexibility of finding another rhyme, another way to express something, of starting in a different place, and being able to play with words, sentences, synonyms, expressions and verses in order to accommodate and meet the exigencies of rhyme and rhythm. On the other hand, one must also have the rigidity and discipline to remain faithful to the text, to convey the same ideas and messages as the author and to render the text as meaningful to one's contemporary readers as Molière was to his seventeenth century French audience. But sometimes, when the translator is trying to make the text speak to his/her contemporaries, he/she must take liberties and depart from the original. The opposite case—too literal a translation—may, on the other hand, pay too much attention to the letter of the text, and lose its flavor. In all the time I've been working on this translation I've come to realize that, perhaps the ideal translation is a balance of all the elements I mentioned before. In the case of a play in rhymed verse, two elements are already fixed. This makes it clearer to translate, even though it is much more restricting than prose. Between the fixed elements of rhyme and rhythm, one must juggle the faithfulness to the text and the liberties of idiomatic expressions taken to render the spirit of the original in another language and another time.

I am truly grateful to Professor Emeritus Philippa Wehle of Purchase College, SUNY, for teaching the French Translation Workshop where I first came into contact with Molière's work by translating one scene from "L'école des femmes" as practice, during my senior year at Purchase College. It was because of Professor Wehle and her wonderfully inspiring class that I decided to translate the whole play as my senior project. The translation was awarded the language and culture prize of excellence at Purchase that year, and, throughout the years, I have been asked by Purchase College faculty, such as Drama Studies Professor Kay Capo, to allow the use of it in her classes. Translating "L'école des femmes" has been a rewarding experience on many levels: from the actual process to its growth beyond the status of graduation project to bloom into the classroom as a course material at my alma mater—where it all began.

Maria-Cristina Necula

FOREWORD

To translate a masterpiece is a challenge for the best of translators. Translating a masterpiece written in Alexandrine verse ranks at the top on a scale of difficulty. And when it is a translation of a play, in this case Molière's *L'École des femmes*, the challenge is not only to make the audience laugh but to make sure that the actors are comfortable speaking the words the translator has chosen. Maria-Cristina Necula has more than succeeded on all fronts. She has found creative ways to solve the most daunting problems while avoiding the pitfalls of remaining too close to the text.

I admire Cristina's courage. She fearlessly tackles problems of rhythms, rimes, transitions and timing, especially the timing of Molière's comic effects at the ends of his lines, and she consistently comes up with imaginative solutions. But these are only some of the problems the translator of a seventeenth century classic encounters. The differences in speech and choice of words between the elegant phrasings of the more sophisticated Chrysalde and the prosaic mutterings of Arnolphe, a provincial bourgeois, not to mention the pedantic expressions of the notary and the colorful chatter of the servants, are equally challenging. Cristina beautifully meets these challenges as well.

Most importantly, perhaps, is the question of the texture of a translation, the manner in which the threads of meaning are interwoven in a piece. In her sensitive and fine translation of Molière's *L'École des femmes*, Maria-Cristina

Necula has captured the texture of Molière's comedic universe. Needless to say, this is no small achievement.

Philippa Wehle, *Professor Emeritus of French Language and Culture and Drama Studies, Purchase College, State University of New York, and Chevalier in the Order of Arts and Letters*

Cast Of Characters

ARNOLPHE, also known as Sir de Stump

AGNES, a young, innocent girl raised by Arnolphe; in love with Horace

HORACE, young man in love with Agnes

ALAIN, peasant, Arnolphe's butler

GEORGETTE, peasant woman, Arnolphe's housekeeper

CHRYSALDE, Arnolphe's friend

ENRIQUE, Chrysalde's brother-in-law

ORONTE, Horace's father, and Arnolphe's good friend

THE NOTARY

ACT ONE

Scene I

Chrysalde, Arnolphe

Chrysalde:	So, you say you've returned to ask her for her hand?
Arnolphe:	I want to get it done by morning as I planned.
Chrysalde:	Well, here we are alone, no one can overhear;
	We can discuss your case openly, without fear.
	In friendship shall I then open my heart to you?
	For your own sake I fear what you're about to do.
	Just look at it from every angle that you can:
	Taking a wife, for you, is truly a rash plan.
Arnolphe:	That may well be, my friend. But your fears for me
	Seem to be based on your wretched reality,
	And having felt a cuckold's horns upon your head,
	You think that they belong to all men who are wed.
Chrysalde:	Here only fate decides, and no one can resist.
	It's plain stupidity, in caution to persist.
	What makes me afraid is the way that you sneer
	At all unfortunate husbands of whom you hear.
	In short, you know there is no cuckold, great or small,
	That can escape your jests, you criticize them all;
	Your greatest pleasure is, wherever you may be,
	To expose secret plots and intrigues blatantly . . .
Arnolphe:	So? Is there another town in which you can find
	Husbands like our own, so patient and resigned?
	Don't we see examples here of every sort
	Who're welcomed at home by a wife and her escort?

One has much wealth; his wife, so sweet and yet so bold,

Distributes it to those who'll crown him a cuckold.

The other, still a wretch, but with a kinder fate,

Observing gifts presented to his lifelong mate,

Maintains his peace of mind free from all jealousy,

For she says her virtue attracts this gallantry.

One shouts and makes much noise, but it does him no good.

Another calmly lets things happen as they would.

And when a gallant squire calls on the one he loves,

In all propriety, he takes his hat and gloves.

One wife skilled, as all are, at making false confessions

Faithfully tells her spouse of so-and so's attentions.

Thus she calms him, and he can pity or disdain

The poor man for his efforts which are not in vain.

Another, to explain why she's so prosperous,

Says she has been at games of luck, victorious.

Her husband, not thinking of just how she excels,

Praises God for her luck, meanwhile her fortune swells.

With so many subjects for comedy around,

There's plenty to make fun of. Am I not allowed

To laugh at these poor fools . . .

Chrysalde: Don't get carried away!

Who laughs at another might be laughed at someday.

I hear people talk about what's on their mind,

Discussing what goes on, as a way to unwind.

But whatever they say is happening in town,

Nobody sees me try to put anyone down.

I'm discreet even though there are times when I do

Condemn our tolerance for such plots, just like you.

I don't plan to suffer like other married men

Who peacefully accept this special regimen.

However, I don't put my purpose to the test

By boasting; I know that he who laughs last, laughs best.

And so, a man should never swear in advance

What he will do or not in such a circumstance.

As for me, if my fate should treat me in this way,

If I'll meet with disgrace, the price I'll have to pay

Would be smaller since I've behaved so decently.

People would laugh but they would do it secretly,

And maybe, as tribute to my wise modesty,

Some gentle souls might feel sympathy towards me.

But with you, dear friend, it's just the opposite;

You're taking a hell of a risk, I must admit.

Since with your sneering tongue, you have, time and again,

Exposed, slandered, laughed at all luckless married men

And, like a devil roused, mocked them without pity,

If you meet in your path with infidelity,

You will become yourself subject for comedy;

At all cross-roads you'll be run down by mockery,

And . . .

Arnolphe: For God's sake, my friend, if you're worried, don't be!

No one is smart enough to make a fool of me.

Besides, I know the tricks and all the subtle ways

That our women employ to set us up these days.

They can dupe anyone with skillful artistry.

But I made quite certain that won't happen to me!

The girl I will marry, in all her innocence,

Will protect my forehead from harmful influence.

Chrysalde: You think a simple girl or, in a word, a fool . . .

Arnolphe: It's the way to marry to avoid ridicule.

I know your better half is virtuous indeed,

But a clever woman is an evil breed.

And I know what it costs some men to have married

Smart women. Now they wish they were dead and buried.

Me? Wedding someone with intellectual talents

Who'd talk of nothing but the clubs that she frequents,

Who would write sweet nonsense in verses and in prose

While high-minded *marquis*, like bees near a rose,

Would swarm 'round her? And I, husband of the great Dame—

A saint with no faithful worshippers to my name?

No, I refuse to wed a complicated brain.

A woman who can write is a guaranteed pain!

I don't want a wife whose mind is too sublime,

She should not even be aware that words can rhyme.

And if she ever plays that rhyme-game I dislike

And, being her turn, they ask her: "What would you like?"

I want her, as a child, to say: "A cream tart, please."

In short, I want a wife who will not be at ease

In high society. All that she needs to know

Is how to spin, to pray, to love me and to sew.

Chrysalde:	Then it is your fancy to have a stupid wife?
Arnolphe:	Not only stupid but ugly, to save my life,
	Rather than a beauty, clever and efficient.
Chrysalde:	Beauty and brilliance . . .
Arnolphe:	Honesty's sufficient.
Chrysalde:	But, after all, how could a simple fool know what
	Honesty is, and how would she understand that?
	Not to mention the fact that your whole future life
	Will be a dreadful bore alongside such a wife.
	Do you think that marriage in this way will ensure

Your safety from what many have had to endure?

A clever woman might betray her faith one day,

But it's because she wants and dares to act this way.

Meanwhile a fool can stray from the right path as well

Not wishing to do so, not knowing how she fell.

Arnolphe: Fine argument. But now I'll gladly take this chance

To quote from Rabelais, Pantagruel's response

To Panurge: "Just try to convince me not to wed

A fool. Preach till the end of time; when all is said

And done, you will be simply astonished to see

That nothing you have said would ever persuade me."

Chrysalde: I won't say any more.

Arnolphe: Each man plays his own game.

In marriage, as in all, my rules remain the same.

I'm rich enough, I think, to pick the type of wife

Who owns nothing and will depend on me for life.

Thus she will never claim a right to property

Or even noble birth; she will belong to me.

She was four years old when I first noticed her,

I was captivated by her sweet, kind manner.

Seeing her mother crushed by poverty and hardship

Gave me the thought to ask for the girl's guardianship.

The good peasant woman, finding out my intent

To relieve her of her charge, was very content.

Thus in a small convent far from all temptation,

I closely supervised the girl's education

By creating a set of rules, so well defined,

Meant to preserve the simplicity of her mind.

Thank God, my system proved to be a great success;

Though she has grown, her mind is pure nevertheless.

So simple is she that I've blessed Heaven each day

For creating a bride according to my way.

So one day, from the convent I took her away.

But since my home is open to people every day,

I took all precautions and had her live alone

In a place no one knows—this other house I own.

And to preserve unspoiled her sweet purity,

I've picked for her two servants as naive as she.

You'll ask me: "Why this story?" So that you understand

How much work and planning marriage and love demand.

And finally, my faithful friend, I must request

That you come dine with us tonight, and do your best

To examine closely my lovely future bride

And tell me if my choice may not be justified.

Chrysalde: I accept.

Arnolphe: You'll be able, after meeting her,

To judge the innocence of her demeanor.

Chrysalde: As for her innocence, everything you've told me

Is . . .

Arnolphe: The truth surpasses my story, as you'll see.

The things she says sometimes fill my heart with delight;

So naive are they that I laugh with all my might.

The other day—and now you'll really be amused—

She came to me seeming just utterly confused,

And asked me in a way so innocent and dear,

If the children one has are made through the ear.

Chrysalde: I'm so glad, Sir Arnolphe . . .

Arnolphe: I say, you have no shame!

Why do you keep calling me by my former name?

Chrysalde:	Oh, I forgot again! I guess I prefer it
	To Sir de Stump; it's just easier, I admit.
	Tell me what in the devil's name possessed you to
	Unbaptize yourself at the age of forty-two,
	Giving yourself a title of nobility
	From an old tree-trunk on your farm property?
Arnolphe:	Not only has that farm been called this way for years,
	But Sir de Stump sounds much more pleasant to my ears.
Chrysalde:	Can you renounce that name, your father's legacy,
	To take one which is nothing but pure fantasy?
	Yet, from what I hear, it's become the new trend.
	And without comparing or wishing to offend,
	All this reminds me of Big Pierre, a peasant who
	Owned a small piece of land—of an acre or two—
	And, having dug around his farm a muddy ditch,
	From Pierre to Lord Island he made a happy switch.
Arnolphe:	You could do without examples of this kind!
	Sir de Stump is my name; and why should you mind?
	It's legal, I like it, and you should realize
	It would be impolite to call me otherwise.
Chrysalde:	However, most people have trouble with this name.
	I've noticed your letters are still addressed the same . . .
Arnolphe:	I can put up with it from those who do not know;
	But you . . .
Chrysalde:	I understand. No need to scold me so.
	I'll forget your old name. From now on I intend
	To call you Sir de Stump as you wish, my good friend.
Arnolphe:	Farewell then, Sir Chrysalde. I'll knock here to say
	That I am back again and bid them a good day.
Chrysalde	*(leaving)*: I really think he's lost what was left of his mind.

Arnolphe   *(alone)*: He seems stuck when it comes to matters of this kind.

It's funny to observe how such closed-minded passion

Makes one see things only in a certain fashion!

(knocks at gate)

Hello!

Scene II

Alain, Georgette, Arnolphe

Alain: Who's there?

Arnolphe: Open up! *(aside.)* I can already sense

Their joy at seeing me after ten days' absence.

Alain: Who is it?

Arnolphe: Me.

Alain: Georgette!

Georgette: What?

Alain: Go open below.

Georgette: You go.

Alain: No, you do it.

Georgette: For God's sake, I won't go!

Alain: I'm not going either.

Arnolphe: What a welcome I get!

I'm shut out! Hey, Alain, open up please! Georgette!

Georgette: Who's there?

Arnolphe: Your master.

Georgette: Alain!

Alain: What?

Georgette: Go! It's him!

Open now!

Alain: You do it.

Georgette: The fire's growing dim.

Alain: Well, I'm keeping my sparrow out of the cat's way.

Arnolphe: Whoever doesn't open this door right away

               Will not get any supper for at least four days.

               Ha!

Georgette: Why have you come too when I open always?

Alain: Why you instead of me? I know the tricks you play!

Georgette: Move, get away from there.

Alain: Oh no, you get away.

Georgette: I want to open it.

Alain: That is what I want too.

Georgette: You won't.

Alain: You won't either.

Georgette: Well, then neither will you.

Arnolphe: I do believe no one is as patient as I . . .

Alain   *(entering)*:

               I opened it, Sir.

Georgette   *(entering)*:   No! he didn't. What a lie!

               I did it.

Alain: If Master were not here, I swear

               I'd . . .

Arnolphe   *(receiving a blow from Alain)*:

                    Damn it!

Alain: Sorry, Sir.

Arnolphe: You clumsy fool! Beware!

Alain: It was her fault too, Sir . . .

Arnolphe: Just shut up, both of you.

               Leave all nonsense aside, and answer quick and true.

               Alain, while I was far away, how did things go?

Alain:	Well, Sir we've . . . Sir, we've been . . . Thank God we were . . . you know . . .

(Arnolphe removes Alain's hat three times, the latter keeps putting it back on)

We did . . .

Arnolphe: Where did you learn, you insolent blockhead,
To speak to me wearing your hat upon your head?

Alain: You are right, Sir. I'm wrong.

Arnolphe   *(to Alain)*:   Tell Agnes to come down.

(to Georgette):

When I left, was she sad? Miserable? Did she frown?

Georgette: Oh, no.

Arnolphe: No?

Georgette: I mean . . . yes!

Arnolphe: Why then?

Georgette: Because she thought
You'd be back anytime. And when our ears caught
The sound of horses, mules or donkeys in the street,
Thinking it might be you, she'd jump up from her seat.

Scene III

Agnes, Alain, Georgette, Arnolphe

Arnolphe: Her work in hand! That looks like a good sign to me.

              Well, Agnes, I've returned from my trip, as you see.

              Tell me, aren't you pleased?

Agnes: Oh yes, Sir! Thank the Lord.

Arnolphe: I am pleased too. This joy is a deserved reward.

              So, have you been as well as you appear to be?

Agnes: Yes, except for last night when the fleas bothered me.

Arnolphe: Well, soon you'll have someone to chase them all away.

Agnes: I'll be so glad.

Arnolphe: I know, my little protégée.

              What are you making there?

Agnes: Some bonnets for myself.

              Your night shirts and night caps are done. You'll see yourself.

Arnolphe: Ah, that's great! Now go back upstairs and wait there.

              I'll come soon. First, there are some things I must prepare.

              Then we need to discuss an important subject.

              (alone): Heroines of our time, ladies of intellect,

              Vendors of tenderness and feelings so sublime,

              I defy all at once your books and your sweet rhyme,

              Your poetic letters. How can your skills compare

              To this sweet ignorance, honest, decent and rare?

Scene IV

Horace, Arnolphe

Arnolphe:	One shouldn't be dazzled just by wealth, I admit,
	Provided that honor . . . What do I see? Is it? . . .
	No. Actually, it is . . . No, can't be. Yes! Dear boy . . .
	Hor . . .
Horace:	Sir . . .
Arnolphe:	Horace.
Horace:	Arnolphe.
Arnolphe:	Such unexpected joy!
	How long have you been here?
Horace:	Just nine days.
Arnolphe:	Is that true?
Horace:	When I arrived I stopped by, in vain, to see you.
Arnolphe:	I was in the country.
Horace:	You'd left two days before.
Arnolphe:	Oh, how fast children grow! I'm amazed evermore
	To see you as you are, when not so long ago
	You were as tall as from the ground to here, or so.
Horace:	That's right.
Arnolphe:	But tell me please: how's your father these days
	Oronte, my good friend whom I honor and praise?
	What has he been up to? Still cheerful and strong?
	He knows his life has been my concern for so long.
	It's been four years since we've seen each other last;
	We never even wrote, the time flew by so fast!
Horace:	He is, Mr. Arnolphe, happier than we are.
	He wrote you this letter. I've had no news so far

Until today—he writes that he is coming here

And the reason for it is not completely clear.

Perhaps you know that a citizen of this town,

Having in fourteen years gained much wealth and renown,

Will return from America this very week.

Arnolphe: Do you, by any chance, know this man's name?

Horace: Enrique.

Arnolphe: Don't know him.

Horace: My father writes me of his return

As if, to me, this ought to be of some concern.

Then he writes that he'll meet this Enrique on the way

To settle something which the letter doesn't say.

(Horace gives Oronte's letter to Arnolphe)

Arnolphe: I'll be happy to see your father, that great man.

I will welcome and treat him as best as I can.

(after having read the letter):

There is no need though for such letters between friends,

They shouldn't waste much time with useless compliments;

And even if he hadn't written me a word,

I would have lent you all you need, don't be absurd!

Horace: I'll need to take advantage of your kind intent;

With a hundred pistoles I'd be more than content.

Arnolphe: By God, to be of service is my greatest joy.

I even have the cash with me, my dear boy.

You can keep the purse too.

Horace: But wait . . .

(wants to give Arnolphe an I.O.U.)

Arnolphe: Oh, put it down!

Well now, go on, tell me how do you find this town?

Horace: Crowded; but with such fine buildings and monuments

	And, I assume, quite rich in its divertissements.
Arnolphe:	Here a man has as much fun as he desires,
	Especially if he's one of those "gallant" squires.
	This town is favorable to their gallantry
	Since our women are skilled masters of coquetry.
	Brunettes as well as blondes are equally inclined
	To be polite and sweet; their husbands too are kind!
	It is a royal sport, a comical display,
	Observing it keeps me laughing more every day.
	Perhaps you have yourself broken a heart or two.
	Hasn't luck come your way in some sweet rendezvous?
	You are the type that makes a husband a cuckold,
	And your good looks are worth much more than pure gold.
Horace:	I will not hide the truth from you, and to confess,
	I must say that in love I've met with much success
	Right in this town. And since we're friends I'll tell you how.
Arnolphe	(aside): Wonderful! I can't wait to hear this one now!
	One more funny story to add to my collection.
Horace:	But please be discreet for the sake of protection.
Arnolphe:	Oh!
Horace:	You know that in this kind of circumstance
	An uncovered secret will destroy love's chance.
	I will confess to you—and you know I'm no liar—
	That a local beauty has set my soul on fire.
	My attentions have had, from the start, such success
	That to her heart I have easily gained access.
	I do not mean to boast or do her any wrong
	But my position is, without a doubt, quite strong.
Arnolphe	(laughing): Who is she?

| Horace | *(pointing to Agnes' house)*: A sweet thing who lives just over |

Horace   *(pointing to Agnes' house)*: A sweet thing who lives just over
          there
          In that house with red walls; her beauty is quite rare.
          She is really naive because of the man who
          Foolishly has hidden her from the world's view.
          The ignorance he keeps her in will bring him harm
          For it shines within her as a ravishing charm,
          Bringing out her sweetness, tenderness, innocence—
          Everything against which a heart has no defense.
          But perhaps you've seen her, this bright young star of love,
          Adorned with divine charms, delicate as a dove.
          Her name is Agnes.

Arnolphe *(aside)*:   Ah! I'm dying!

Horace: And his name
          Is something like de Plump or de Clump. What a shame
          I cannot remember; I didn't care for it.
          They say he's rich but he lacks common sense and wit;
          Actually, they say, he's quite ridiculous.
          Do you know him?

Arnolphe *(aside)*:   This pill is rather poisonous!

Horace: You have nothing to say?

Arnolphe: Ah! Yes, I know him, but . . .

Horace: He's really crazy, right?

Arnolphe: Oh! . . .

Horace: What did you say? . . . What?
          "Oh"?! That means "yes"? He is jealous too, isn't he?
          A fool? They didn't lie, describing him to me.
          In short, the lovely Agnes has enslaved my heart.
          She is a precious gem, a superb work of art,
          And it would be a sin if this beauty, so rare,

Stays in that man's power, he's strange beyond compare.

My efforts and sweet vows of love will win her soon;

She will be mine in spite of that jealous buffoon.

The money I've borrowed from you with such boldness

Will help me execute my plan with some success.

You know that however strong our efforts may be

To accomplish something, money's the only key.

This sweet metal can intoxicate a man's brain

And, in love as in war, help him conquer and reign.

You seem a bit distressed. Perhaps you disagree

With what I have in mind. If you do, please tell me.

Arnolphe: No, I was just thinking . . .

Horace: This talk has bored you then.

Farewell; I'll stop by soon to say thank you again.

Arnolphe *(thinking he is alone)*:

Ah! must it . . .

Horace *(returning)*: Once again, please try to be discreet,

And don't let my secret escape out on the street.

Arnolphe *(thinking he is alone again)*:

What I'm feeling inside . . .

Horace *(returning)*: And above all, don't tell

My father. He would make my life a living hell.

Arnolphe *(expecting Horace to return again)*:

Oh! . . .

(alone): Oh! how I've suffered through that conversation!

No soul has ever felt such painful vexation.

With what an extreme haste, and how imprudently

He came to tell his story! And to whom? . . . To me!

Since he doesn't know about my other name,

The fool confessed right to the man he wants to frame!

But though I was in pain, I should have kept my head

And gotten out of him all he has not yet said.

I should have pushed his indiscretion to the edge

And found out to what extent they fulfilled their pledge.

He's not too far. I'll try to catch him if I can,

To learn all the details of their evil plan.

I fear a new misfortune torturing my mind.

Why do we always seek more than we wish to find?

ACT TWO

Scene I

Arnolphe: Now that I think about it, I really must say:

I am better off to have lost him on the way;

Because it would have been very hard otherwise

To hide my pressing torment from his watchful eyes.

He would have discovered my consuming care

Of which I would not want him to become aware.

But I am not a man who will be taken in,

Leaving the way open for that young fop to win;

I'm going to stop him and find out for a fact

Just how far they have pushed their mysterious pact.

My honor is very important in my life

And I already look at this girl as my wife.

Any mistake she makes can cover me with shame

And what she's done so far might spoil my good name.

Oh, fatal departure! Unlucky trip, curse you!

(He knocks at the gate)

Scene II

Alain, Georgette, Arnolphe

Alain: Ah! Sir, this time . . .

Arnolphe: Quiet! Now come here, you two.

Let's go! Move it! Come on! Come here now, I say.

Georgette: Ah, Sir! My blood turns cold to see you act this way.

Arnolphe: So this is how you two obey me when I'm gone:

Plotting to betray me, fool me, and lead me on!

Georgette *(falling on her knees in front of Arnolphe)*:

Oh! don't eat me alive, I implore you, master.

Alain *(aside)*: Some mad dog must have bit him to cause this disaster.

Arnolphe *(aside)*: Ouf! I can't talk, I have a dreadful premonition.

I can't breathe and these clothes worsen my condition.

(to Alain and Georgette):

You cursed scoundrels! I know that you did allow

A man to come . . .

(to Alain who is trying to run away):

　　　　Aha! You want to run off now!

(to Georgette):

You must tell me at once . . .

(to Alain):　　　　If you move . . .

(to both):　　　　　　I want you

To tell me the truth . . . uh . . . I demand that you two . . .

(Alain and Georgette get up and try to escape again.)

If anyone moves now, I'll send him to his grave!

I want you to tell me how did that man, that knave,

Get inside my house, huh? Speak up! Hurry! Be quick!

Wake up and talk!

Alain and Georgette:　　　　Ah! Ah!

Georgette *(falling on her knees again)*: My heart has stopped. I'm sick.

Alain *(falling on his knees too)*:

I'm dying.

Arnolphe *(aside)*: I'm sweating; I need to get some air.

I must try to cool off; I'll take a walk somewhere.

When he was just a boy, who would have ever guessed

That he'd turn out like this. God, my heart's too distressed!

I think it would be best if I could succeed

To get from her own lips the details I need.

I must soothe the resentment that tears me apart.

Take it easy now. Have patience, my poor heart!

(to Alain and Georgette):

Get up and go inside; have Agnes come down here.

No, stop! *(aside)*: That way she'll be less surprised, I fear;

They'd warn her of my troubled state, without a doubt.

I'd better go myself and tell her to come out.

(to Alain and Georgette):

You wait for me right here.

Scene III

Alain, Georgette

Georgette:	My God! He's terrible!
	His looks aroused in me a fear so horrible;
	I've never seen a more hideous Christian man.
Alain:	I told you he'd be angry at that gentleman.
Georgette:	But what the hell is it that makes him order us
	To keep our mistress locked? And he makes such a fuss!
	Why does he hide her from the world? It's just too queer
	How he never allows anyone to come near.
Alain:	Oh, it's because this would arouse his jealousy.
Georgette:	But what's the reason why he thinks like that, tell me!
Alain:	Oh well, the reason is . . . he's jealous. Understand?
Georgette:	Yes, but why does his temper get so out of hand?
Alain:	That's because jealousy . . . now listen well, Georgette,
	Is a thing . . . something that can make anyone fret

And chase away all those who come near his place.

I'll give you a comparison just as a base

For your understanding. Tell me, isn't it true

That, when you are eating and enjoying your stew,

If some hungry being should come and eat from it,

You'd want to beat him up for you'd have such a fit.

Georgette: Yes, that I understand.

Alain: Well, now you have a clue

About the way things are. The woman is man's stew;

When, now and then, he sees other men try to stick

Their fingers in his stew, it makes him really sick

With a terrible rage, a fury he can't tame.

Georgette: Yes, but then why isn't everyone else the same?

Some men seem so happy to have their wives go out

With those fine gentlemen; they don't complain or shout.

Alain: Because not everyone has such a greedy mind

To keep all for himself.

Georgette: Unless I'm really blind,

I think he's coming back.

Alain: He is; your eyes are good.

Georgette: He looks so sad.

Alain: His troubles have put him in this mood.

Scene IV

Arnolphe, Agnes, Alain, Georgette

Arnolphe   *(aside)*: A Greek once gave Augustus, the famous emperor,

The kind of good advice anyone would wish for:

If something makes us really angry and upset,

We should, before we act, recite the alphabet

In order to allow our anger to subside

So we don't do something rash or undignified.

With Agnes, I have put this advice to the test.

I've asked her to come out in order to suggest

That we take a short walk; it's only an excuse

For my suspicious mind to skillfully induce

Her to talk about what I'm dying to hear.

Thus, in probing her heart, things might become more clear.

Come, Agnes.

(to Alain and Georgette): You, go in.

Scene V

Arnolphe, Agnes

Arnolphe: Oh, such a lovely walk.

Agnes: Indeed.

Arnolphe: And such a day.

Agnes: Indeed.

Arnolphe: What news? Please talk.

Agnes: The kitten's dead.

Arnolphe: A pity! But what's new in that?

Everyone is mortal, including a poor cat.

While I was in the country, tell me, did it rain?

Agnes: No.

Arnolphe: Were you bored?

Agnes: Never! Boredom I do disdain.

| Arnolphe: | These past nine or ten days, what have you done, I pray? |

Arnolphe: These past nine or ten days, what have you done, I pray?

Agnes: Six shirts I've made, and also six caps, if I may say.

Arnolphe *(having reflected a while)*:

The world is strange, dear Agnes. You should be aware

That people love to talk, and slander's everywhere.

Some neighbors told me how a young man no one knew

Came to the house while I was far away from you.

His glances and his words, I heard, you did endure;

But slander such as this is wicked talk, I'm sure.

Thus, I wanted to bet that their words were false news . . .

Agnes: For God's sake, do not bet: you would certainly lose.

Arnolphe: What? Then it's true that a man . . . ?

Agnes: Yes, of course it's true.

He almost didn't move from here, I swear to you.

Arnolphe *(aside, softly)*:

This oath she made just now with such sincerity

Is proof enough at least of her pure honesty.

(aloud.) If my memory's still good, I'm sure I told you, dear,

That you were not to have any visitors here.

Agnes: Oh, yes; but you don't know the reason why he came,

And, being in my place, you would have done the same.

Arnolphe: Maybe; but I would like to know this story too.

Agnes: It's so astonishing, you won't believe it's true.

Sitting on the terrace, sewing in the cool breeze,

I saw someone moving among the near-by trees:

An elegant young man who, setting eyes on me,

Greeted me with a bow as humble as can be.

As for my part, not lacking in civility,

I curtsied with the same proper humility.

But all of a sudden, he bowed to me once more;

I curtsied in return just like I'd done before.

And he, a third time, bowed to me in the same way,

Thus I too, a third time, curtsied without delay.

So he went back and forth, and when by me he passed,

Bow after bow followed, each better than the last.

My eyes were glued to him as he kept walking by,

Each bow received a curtsy as a fair reply;

So endless did this seem that, if night didn't fall,

I don't think it would have ever ended at all

For I couldn't have stopped, I feared what he'd say:

I, less civil than he? The thought caused me dismay.

Arnolphe: Well done.

Agnes: The morning after, at our gate I met

A shriveled old woman who seemed a bit upset.

She spoke to me thus: "Child, may the good Lord bless you

And may He keep your charms forever fresh and new!

Heaven did not bestow on you beauty and charm

So that you would use them in order to cause harm.

You must know how deeply you have wounded someone

Whose heart is the saddest of hearts under the sun."

Arnolphe   *(aside)*: Ah! damned servant of hell! abominable shrew!

Agnes: 'I hurt someone!' said I, shocked, for I knew not who.

"Yes", said she, "but not 'hurt', wounded—I'd rather say.

It was the young man whom you saw just yesterday."

'Dear God, how could I have, without any intention,

Caused him harm of such incredible dimension?'

"Well, it was not your fault, your eyes must take the blame,

Their glances and the stab of arrows are the same."

'My God!' said I, 'what an unparalleled surprise:

To think that I can cause such harm with my own eyes!'

"Yes", she replied, "your eyes can deadly ills bestow;

Dear, they contain a poison of which you don't know.

In brief, the poor man thus suffers terribly,

And if it happens that, through your harsh cruelty,

You would refuse to help a soul in despair

His grave you might as well, within two days prepare."

'Good Lord! my pain would then be great beyond belief.

What does he ask of me? How could I bring relief?'

"My child", she told me, "he only hopes for the right

To see you and to speak with you, this way you might,

Through your eyes only, stop his ruin, for you know

Your eyes can heal the pain they've caused hours ago."

'Alas!' I cried, 'then, if this is the case, he should

Come visit me right here as often as he could.'

Arnolphe	*(aside)*: Ah! poisoner of hearts! Damned witch, may you be cursed!

For your kind acts by hell may you be reimbursed.

Agnes:	So he came to see me to heal his malady.

I did the proper thing, don't you agree with me?

For how could I have had the conscience to deny

The help he asked me for, and coldly let him die?

I, who pity all those who are oppressed or sick,

And cry each time I see anyone kill a chick?

Arnolphe	*(aside)*: All that she says is proof of her soul's innocence,

And I can only blame my imprudent absence

Which left her moral goodness without any guide,

Prey to those seducers so skilled and evil-eyed.

I fear that the rascal, not having any shame,

Has pushed things far beyond a light innocent game.

Agnes:	What's the matter? You seem a little irritated.
	Was there something wrong in what I just narrated?
Arnolphe:	No, no. But tell me more; I'm curious, my dear,
	To know how the young man spent his visits here.
Agnes:	Oh, if you could have seen his unsurpassed delight;
	As soon as he walked in, he became all right,
	And the gift he brought me: a beautiful *cassette*,
	And the money he gave to Alain and Georgette.
	You would have loved him too, I know that for a fact . . .
Arnolphe:	But when he was alone with you, how did he act?
Agnes:	He swore he felt for me a love beyond compare.
	Oh, I had never heard such kind words, I declare,
	So unequaled by any said to me before;
	Each sweet, enchanted word made me wish for more.
	They brought me a pleasure I could hardly contain
	And stirred inside my soul something I can't explain.
Arnolphe	*(aside)*: O horrid inspection of a cursed mystery,
	Where only the inspector suffers this misery!
	(to Agnes): Besides the lovely words that he spoke to you,
	Were there not as well a few caresses too?
Agnes:	Oh many! He would take my hands, my arms, and then
	He would kiss them all over again and again.
Arnolphe:	And, Agnes, didn't he take something else as well?
	(seeing her confused):
	Ouf!
Agnes:	Well, he . . .
Arnolphe:	Yes?
Agnes:	Took . . .
Arnolphe:	Oh!
Agnes:	My . . .

Arnolphe: What?

Agnes: I dare not tell

Because I am afraid you'll be angry with me.

Arnolphe: No.

Agnes: Yes, you will.

Arnolphe: God, no!

Agnes: Then swear you won't be.

Arnolphe: I swear.

Agnes: He took my . . . Oh, you'll be furious.

Arnolphe: No.

Agnes: Yes.

Arnolphe: No, no! Damn it! you're too mysterious!

What did he take then?

Agnes: He . . .

Arnolphe *(aside)*: I suffer horribly.

Agnes: He took . . . He took the ribbon you had given me.

To tell you the whole truth, I couldn't stop him though.

Arnolphe *(recovering his breath)*:

Forget the ribbon now. What I wanted to know

Was if he did anything else you can recall.

Agnes: What? Does one do other things?

Arnolphe: No, no. Not at all.

But, in order to heal his painful malady,

Didn't he ask you for another remedy?

Agnes: No. But you can be sure that if he had done so,

In order to help him, I wouldn't have said "no".

Arnolphe *(aside, softly)*: Thank Heaven that this time I got off really

cheap.

If I slip one more time, then I'll deserve to weep.

Hush! *(aloud.)* Agnes, your innocence is the one to blame.

I won't scold you; what's done is done all the same.

I can see how the *gallant* plans to have his fun:

He flatters and deceives you, then laughs at what he's done.

Agnes:	Oh, no! he told me so a dozen times or more.
Arnolphe:	Ah! but I'm sure his words have been false before.

Well, anyway, Agnes, it's time for you to know

That if you accept gifts from any fine young beau,

If you allow their chatter to tickle your soul,

And passively let them kiss you, losing control;

It is a mortal sin, the biggest of its kind.

Agnes: A sin, you say? But why? Tell me, if you don't mind.

Arnolphe: It's an unwritten law that has, since long, stated

That these acts make Heaven really infuriated.

Agnes: Infuriated? Why? Why should Heaven be mad

At something so pleasant and sweet, not at all bad?

I really admire the pleasure all this brings;

I never knew before about such lovely things.

Arnolphe: Yes, it's a great pleasure to feel a sweet caress

And listen to a promise filled with tenderness;

But one must enjoy this in a rightful way

And, to erase the guilt, get married right away.

Agnes: So, if one is married, it's no longer a crime?

Arnolphe: No.

Agnes: Then let me marry. Now is the perfect time.

Arnolphe: If you desire it, my dear, I do too.

I've returned, as you see, with marriage plans for you.

Agnes: Is it possible?

Arnolphe: Yes.

Agnes: You'll bring me happiness!

Arnolphe: Yes, marriage will please you, I don't doubt it, Agnes.

Agnes: You want the two of us . . .

Arnolphe: Yes, I certainly do.

Agnes: Oh, how I will caress you if that should come true!

Arnolphe: Why, and I'll do the same to you, right on the spot.

Agnes: I can't tell when people are making fun or not.

                Are you serious then?

Arnolphe: Can't you see it? Yes. Quite.

Agnes: We are to be married?

Arnolphe: Oh, yes.

Agnes: But when?

Arnolphe: Tonight.

Agnes   *(laughing)*: Tonight?

Arnolphe: Yes, yes, tonight. So you're laughing, it seems.

Agnes: Yes.

Arnolphe: To see you happy fulfills all of my dreams.

Agnes: Oh, dear! I will owe you for the rest of my life.

                With him I'll always be happy to be a wife.

Arnolphe: With whom?

Agnes: With . . . the . . .

Arnolphe: With "the"? "The" is not in my plan.

                You are a little hasty in choosing a man.

                There's another husband I have in mind for you.

                And as for Mr. "The", what I want you to do,

                Despite his very painful and quite strange disease,

                Is, from now on, to break all contact with him, please.

                And if he ever comes, his compliments to pay,

                You have to slam the door in his face right away,

                And from your window throw a brick, if he should knock;

                Thus he'll never be seen again around this block.

                Do you understand me? I will be there too,

Hidden in a corner, to watch what you do.

Agnes: Oh dear, he's so handsome! He . . .

Arnolphe: Enough talk from you!

Agnes: I will not have the heart.

Arnolphe: No more noise. You will too!

Go upstairs.

Agnes: But . . . what? . . . You want . . .

Arnolphe: Enough, I say!

I am the master here; I talk and you obey.

ACT III

Scene I

Arnolphe, Agnes, Alain, Georgette

Arnolphe: Yes, everything went well; I'm happy as can be,

For you two have followed my orders perfectly.

Sending the young seducer on his way, confused.

Things work very well when wise leadership is used.

Your innocence, Agnes, was taken by surprise

And pushed you into something you did not realize.

Had I not interfered you, in your condition,

Would have followed the path to Hell and to perdition.

All *gallants* are the same in the way they behave,

Their ribbons, plumes, ruffles are fashion's latest rave.

They've got long hair, fine teeth, sweet promises to sell

But underneath, their claws are sharp and hidden well.

They're true devils whose jaws are tainted and impure;

Out of a woman's honor they make a cleansing cure.

But, once again, thank God for my devoted care

Which helped you to emerge untouched from this affair.

The way you threw that stone at him a while ago,

Smashing his hopes to bits with a swift, single blow,

Convinces me anew that I should not delay

The wedding I have planned; it must get under way.

But first, before all else, let us sit down a bit

And have a little talk for your own benefit.

A chair here, in the shade.

(to Alain and Georgette): You two better watch out.

Georgette:	Oh, we will remember all your lessons, no doubt.
	That gentleman fooled us and we opened the door
	But . . .
Alain:	If he gets in again, I shall drink no more!
	He's a fool anyway; last time, the dumb ingrate
	Gave us two gold pieces which lacked the proper weight.
Arnolphe:	Buy what I ordered then, for our supper tonight,
	And when you're coming back, don't forget to invite
	The notary who lives on the corner of this street;
	Remind him that we have a contract to complete.

Scene II

Arnolphe, Agnes

Arnolphe:	Agnes, put your work down and listen well, my dear.
	Raise your head, turn to me, and keep your eyes right here
	(puts his finger on his forehead)
	While I'm talking to you. And every word I say
	Must be fixed in your mind and never cast away.
	I am marrying you, and you should bless your fate
	A hundred times each day for getting such a mate.
	Reflect a bit upon your former poverty
	And thus you will admire my generosity
	Which brought you from the state of a poor peasant
	Into the bourgeois class, making your life more pleasant.
	For you will share the bed and love of someone who
	Used to flee from marriage, but has now chosen you
	Despite all the good matches that have come his way;
	The honor he denied them is all yours today.

You should remind yourself that you don't count that much

Without this union whose brilliance is such

That it must inspire and teach you to work hard

To deserve this honor and to keep it unscarred.

Thus, you should know yourself and take good care to

Make me very proud of what I plan to do.

Marriage, dear Agnes, is not some child's play;

Solemn duties await a wife along the way.

To such a noble rank, how can you ever climb

By living so freely and having a good time?

Your sex was made, Agnes, for complete dependence;

The beard has the force in all its resplendence.

Although there are two halves in this society,

Nonetheless, these halves have no equality:

One is supreme, the other—its subordinate,

One will always obey, the other—dominate.

And the obedience that a soldier displays

To his fearless captain who guides him always

Is what the least monk shows to his priest much adored,

The child to his father, the servant to his lord.

But this doesn't come close to the docility,

And the obedience, and the humility,

And the profound respect that a woman must bring

In marriage to her man, her master, lord, and king.

Whenever he bestows on her a serious glance,

She must, dutifully, lower her eyes at once

And never even dare to look him in the face

Till he, through a kind look offers her his sweet grace.

The women of today misunderstand all this;

Don't follow in their footsteps, you'll be led amiss.

Don't ever imitate those villainous coquettes

Whose pranks make the town ring with outrageous vignettes.

Beware of Satan who will attack your soul

Through the words of some fop who knows how to cajole.

Think that you'll soon become my other half. Beware,

Thus it is my honor which I leave in your care.

This honor is fragile and easy to be hurt;

It's no joking matter, so I will advert

To those cauldrons boiling in Hell's eternal blaze

Into which fall all those women of evil ways.

What I've told you so far is not some song-and-dance,

They're lessons for your heart, and they'll truly enhance

Your innate purity. If you follow them right,

Your soul, like a lily, will be clean, fresh and white.

But if it slips away from honor's path, your soul

Will certainly become black as the blackest coal.

You'll be for everyone a horror on display,

And one day you'll become the devil's greatest prey

For all eternity, to boil down in Hell.

May God help you escape such a fate, Mademoiselle.

Now curtsy for me, please. As in a convent school

The novice knows by heart the office and each rule,

In entering marriage, a bride should do the same.

In my pocket I have a book of much acclaim

To teach you the duties of a wife from the start;

I don't know the writer, but he's got a good heart;

And I want this to be the only book you'll need.

Here. Let's take a look to see how well you read.

Agnes   *(reads)*:

THE MARRIAGE MAXIMS OR DUTIES OF A MARRIED WOMAN
—WITH DAILY EXERCISES—

Maxim One

When a matrimonial bed

Welcomes a woman to stay,

She must get it in her head

That, despite the trend today,

She belongs to one man and she should never stray.

Arnolphe: I will explain later the meaning of all this.

For now, keep on reading, there's nothing we should miss.

Agnes   *(continues)*: *Maxim Two*

Her make-up and her dress

Must show her heedfulness

Of her husband's desire.

He's the only one her beauty will concern,

And it shouldn't count that others spurn

Her ugly or unsuitable attire.

Maxim Three

She should avoid all potions,

Perfumes, pomades, lotions,

Eye shadows, powders which make the complexion bloom.

All these are fatal drugs to honor and duty,

Such fuss over her beauty

Will bring her husband gloom.

Maxim Four

Every time she goes out, as honor will dictate,

Her coif must hide the lure of her ravishing eyes.

For, in order to please her lifelong mate,

She should please no one else, if she is wise.

Maxim Five

Besides those who visit the husband in his house,

The rule is different for his spouse:

She should receive no one; avoid all artifices

Of some gallant "persister"

Who, visiting the missis,

Will upset the mister.

Maxim Six

All men's gifts should enrage

A woman. She must learn

That in this day and age,

The one who gives wants something in return.

Maxim Seven

In her room there will be no writing desk, no shelf

Which will contain paper, ink, pens or pencils.

The husband is the one who'll use these utensils;

If there's need for writing, he'll write it all himself.

Maxim Eight

Evenings in high society,

Reflections of impiety,

Corrupt women's souls again and again.

Such events should be forbidden on the spot,

It's there where they plot

Against poor married men.

Maxim Nine

Women who wish to keep their honor unscarred

Should never touch a playing card,

For it happens in a flash

That the much deceiving game

Can push a woman into shame

When she will stake more than her cash.

Maxim Ten

The virtuous woman skips

The country picnics and the trips

That have become the trend these days.

A prudent mind reports

That, at the end of all these sports,

The husband is the one who pays.

Arnolphe: You'll finish by yourself and I'll explain it all

In a proper fashion. But now I can recall

I have some business to attend to right away;

It won't take very long, but if I should delay

And the notary comes, tell him to wait inside.

Now, go in. Keep this book carefully by your side.

Scene III

Arnolphe: I can't do better than to make this girl my wife.

I'll shape and mold her soul, she will be mine for life.

She's like a piece of wax pliable in my hands,

I can give her the form that my desire commands.

While I was away, her excessive innocence

Could have led us to a horrid consequence.

But to be very honest, I think I prefer

Innocence as the reason why a wife might err.

The cure for such faults is a piece of cake,

Simpletons are easy to teach and to break,

And if they might have strayed from the right path a bit,

A couple of strong words will bring them back to it.

But a clever woman is quite a different kind,

Our gender's dependent on her twisted mind.

When she's up to something, nothing can block her way

And our admonitions are simply cast away.

Her bright mind serves her well in mocking our advices,

It often makes virtues out of her worst vices

And finds many shrewd ways to reach its evil goals;

Its devices can trick even the wisest souls.

It's useless to attempt to defend oneself,

A smart woman who plots is the devil himself.

If her capricious mind decides out of the blue

To destroy our honor, there's nothing we can do.

Many good, honest men could testify to that.

So, my surprised young fool will find himself laughed at

For his big mouth has brought his success to a halt.

And that is every Frenchman's ordinary fault:

When they find success in some affair or other,

Keeping it a secret is an awful bother.

Their vanity charms them, it gets under their skin,

They'd rather hang themselves than keep their secrets in.

Satan must tempt these women, making them insane

Each time they give their hearts to some young scatterbrain

And so . . . But there he is . . . Let us hide our intent

And find out what sorrow makes him so malcontent.

Scene IV

Horace, Arnolphe

Horace:	I've just been by your house, but it seems pretty clear
	That when I call on you, fate wants to interfere.
	But I'll call again soon, maybe I'll find you there.
Arnolphe:	My God! Such customs are quite useless, I declare.
	All these ceremonies irritate me a lot;
	I think that they should be forbidden on the spot.
	So many people caught in this social nonsense
	Waste two-thirds of their time, for they lack common sense.
	(covering himself)
	Let's put our hats back on. Well, so how's your affair?
	Dear Horace, tell me please, did you get anywhere?
	I was a bit distracted by something before,
	But later on I thought about it more and more
	And I admire the speed with which things have progressed.
	I'm really interested to find out all the rest.
Horace:	Dear me! Since I've opened my poor heart to you,
	My love has had a stroke of bad luck through and through.
Arnolphe:	Oh! How come?
Horace:	Cruel fate has caused me a disaster:
	It brought back from the country the young beauty's master.
Arnolphe:	Such bad luck!
Horace:	And there's more as a matter of fact.
	He's found out everything about our secret pact.
Arnolphe:	How the devil did he find out about you two?
Horace:	Well, I'm not really sure, but I know that it's true.
	At the usual time I was ready to call

On my lovely lady, not expecting at all

The change of attitude on the two servants' part;

The bastards blocked the way to my charming sweetheart

And said: "You disturb us, get away from this place!"

And then they rudely slammed the door right in my face.

Arnolphe: In your face!

Horace: In my face.

Arnolphe: That's very rude indeed.

Horace: And through the door I tried to talk to them and plead,

But each time their answer would be loud and clear:

"Our master has forbidden you to come in here."

Arnolphe: They didn't let you in?

Horace: Oh, no! And the disaster

Was that Agnes confirmed the return of her master

By chasing me away in a proud, angry tone

And throwing from her window quite a heavy stone.

Arnolphe: A stone, you said?

Horace: A stone . . . and pretty large in size.

For my sweet attentions I got a lovely prize.

Arnolphe: The devil! Then it was a waste of time, in vain.

Your current situation seems quite inhumane.

Horace: True. His fatal return has brought me much distress.

Arnolphe: I certainly feel bad for you, I must confess.

Horace: He's destroyed everything.

Arnolphe: Yes; it means nothing, though.

You'll surely find a way to recover, I know.

Horace: I need to come up with a shrewd and clever plan

To conquer the alertness of that jealous man.

Arnolphe: That should be easy then. The girl with all her soul

Loves you.

Horace: Definitely.

Arnolphe: So you'll achieve your goal.

Horace: I hope so.

Arnolphe: That big stone might have knocked you out,

But don't let it stun you.

Horace: Oh no, without a doubt.

I understood at once that my good man was there

And, from his hiding place, guided the whole affair.

But what astounded me, it will surprise you too:

Another incident that seemed almost untrue.

That young beauty who looked so simple and naive

Came up with such a plan you would never believe.

Thus it's true that love is one of the best teachers,

It makes us develop unexpected features

And often changes us in an instant or less.

Its lessons can transform one's soul with great success.

It breaks down within us nature's obstacles

And its sudden effects seem like miracles;

It can make a miser very generous,

A coarse, crude man—polite, a coward—valorous.

The most sluggish spirit can learn how to fly

And the most innocent become cunning and sly.

Well, this last miracle happened to Agnes too.

So, she chased me away without much ado

Saying: "Leave! Your visits are not wanted. Good-bye.

I know all you will say and here's my reply."

This stone which surprised you was thrown out in the street

Together with a note, landing right at my feet.

The letter with the stone, the angry words she'd said,

It all amazed me so, confusing my poor head.

After all, wouldn't you be as surprised as me?

Love knows how to sharpen one's mind, don't you agree?

Can one deny its power to truly inspire

Wonders in any heart, through its eternal fire?

So, what do you think of the trick with the letter?

Don't you admire her wit? She couldn't have done better.

Don't you enjoy seeing that angry, jealous fool

Play such a comic role, subject to ridicule?

Well?

Arnolphe: Yes, very much so.

Horace: Then laugh a little bit.

This man who's armed himself with stones like a nitwit

And, hiding in his home, fought bravely from above

As if I wanted to break in and steal my love;

Who, in his strange fear and painful dismay,

Turned all of his household against me right away,

Now becomes the victim of his own arrogance,

Fooled by the girl he keeps in complete ignorance.

As for me, I admit, even though his return

Has, regarding my love, caused me some concern,

It's all so funny that, each time I think of it,

I laugh so hard I fear that my sides will split.

But I see you're not laughing too much, my good man.

Arnolphe: Oh, pardon me. I'm laughing as much as I can.

Horace: Well, since you're my friend, I will show you her letter.

Everything her heart felt, her hand expressed better

Through such sweet, touching words, simple and sincere

Filled with a tenderness so innocent and dear.

In short, this is nature deciding to reveal

The first pangs of love which the heart can't conceal.

Arnolphe	*(aside, softly)*: You rascal, then it pays to have been taught to write
	Despite my orders not to. Oh, I knew I was right!
Horace	*(reading)*: I want to write to you and I find it difficult to begin. I have thoughts that I wish you would know, but I don't know how to tell them to you and I don't trust my own words. As I'm just beginning to realize that I've always been kept in ignorance, I'm afraid to write down something that might not be right, and to say more than I should. The truth is that I don't know what you have done to me, but I'm so angry I could die because of what I'm forced to do against you, it would cause me the greatest pain in the world to lose you, and I would be very pleased to be yours. Maybe there's something wrong in saying that, but I can't stop myself from saying it, and I would like it all to come true, without doing anything wrong. They tell me that all young men are liars, that I shouldn't listen to them, and that all you've told me was to manipulate me; but I assure you that I can't yet see you capable of such things, and I am so touched by your words that I couldn't begin to see them as false. Tell me honestly what is going on, for after all, I am without malice; you would do the greatest wrong in the world in deceiving me, and I think I would die of grief.

Arnolphe: That witch!

Horace: What's wrong?

Arnolphe: Nothing. Just a cough in my throat.

Horace: Tell me, have you ever read a more touching note?

Despite the cursed precautions the tyrant may display

Can a lovelier soul reveal itself this way?

And surely isn't it a punishable crime

To spoil that pure soul whose nature is sublime,

To kill her inner light and young exuberance

By keeping her stifled in utter ignorance?

At last, it seems that love has pierced that dense veil,

And if my lucky stars should help me not to fail,

When I see that scoundrel, that hangman and traitor,

That animal, that brute . . . if I catch him later . . .

Arnolphe: Good-bye.

Horace: What? You're leaving?

Arnolphe: I'm suddenly aware

That I must attend to some urgent affair.

Horace: Perhaps you know someone who might have access to

The house where she is trapped. Please tell me if you do.

I have no scruples left. But what comfort brings

The fact that a good friend can help you with such things.

Everyone in that house behaves just like a spy,

Meanwhile the two servants seem to intensify

Their nasty attitude each time I see them there

And they never tone down their rude words or harsh stare.

I knew an old woman whose superhuman skill

Served me so well at first but then, she became ill

And four days ago, the poor woman died

While I was left alone and dissatisfied.

Couldn't you help me find some other solution?

Arnolphe: No, but you'll do fine without my contribution.

Horace: Bye. You're the only one in which I can confide.

Scene V

Arnolphe   *(alone)*: Never in my whole life was I so mortified!

How hard it was to hide my sharp, violent pain!

A simple innocent with such a clever brain!

Either she lied herself about her innocence

Or Satan filled her soul with a deceiving sense.

Oh, that fatal letter practically left me dead;

The traitor's evil words have crawled into her head,

He has taken control, while I've been cast away

In my deadly anguish and terrible dismay.

Through the theft of her heart my suffering is doubled,

In both honor and love, I am hurt and troubled.

I'm enraged to be robbed of my own position,

Deceived in my prudence and my intuition.

She will be punished for her free love if I wait,

All I must do is leave her to her evil fate

And I will be avenged on her through her own deeds,

But it's so hard to lose what one adores and needs.

God! And I thought so hard before making a choice!

Must I be so entranced by her charms and her voice?

She has no relatives or money on her part.

She betrayed my kindness, my caring, tender heart.

However, I love her even after this trick

So much that, without her, my spirit will be sick.

Fool! Aren't you ashamed? My fury makes me roar,

And I could slap my face a thousand times or more.

I'll go in for a bit, because I'd like to see

What her expression shows after betraying me.

Heavens, let me escape this terrible disgrace;

Or if I can't do that, at least let me save face,

And give me in this hour of calamity

The constancy I see in others around me.

ACT FOUR

Scene I

Arnolphe: I'm having a hard time trying to stand still

And a thousand cares press down upon my will

As I'm figuring out how to put a stop

To the ardent efforts of that silly fop.

The traitress! How she stood and confronted my stare!

For all that she had done, she didn't even care,

And while she pushes me to an early demise,

No one would suspect it, she seems free of vice.

When I saw her, she looked so calm and unashamed

That my whole being was by hot fury enflamed,

And my heart's burning transports never shook me harder

As now when they doubled my amorous ardor.

I was desperate, bitter, angry with her and more,

Yet I'd never seen her so beautiful before;

Her eyes had never stabbed me with a sharper dart,

I'd never felt such urgent desires in my heart.

If I should be disgraced after some episode

Brought on by my sad fate, I'm sure I'll explode.

Aha! I have watched over her education

With all my tenderness, care and dedication,

Having her as my ward since she was a child,

While my most tender hopes in her were reconciled;

Seeing her grow I've felt her charms increase their power.

Have I, for thirteen years, watched her bloom like a flower

So that some crazy boy can come here and propose

And perhaps kidnap her under my very nose

Now that she's practically married to me at last?

No, by God! My young friend, your foolishness is vast.

You have done well, but now, granted the time I'll spend,

I vow to smash your hopes and bring them to an end,

Thus you won't be able to laugh at me at all.

Scene II

The Notary, Arnolphe

Notary:	Ah, there he is! Good day. Sir, I've answered your call;
	I'm here to complete the contract, if I may.
Arnolphe	*(unaware of the notary's presence)*:
	But how can I do it? In the usual way.
Notary:	
Arnolphe	*(believing himself to be alone)*:
	I should think of all the precautions I must take.
Notary:	Everything I'll write down will be for your own sake.
Arnolphe	*(still unaware of the notary's presence)*:
	I must protect myself against any surprise.
Notary:	Leave matters in my hands and I will organize
	Everything as you wish. And do not be afraid;
	You will not sign the contract until the dowry's paid.
Arnolphe	*(still thinking himself alone)*:
	I'm afraid that someone will find out about this;
	I'd be the talk of town, to the gossipers' bliss.
Notary:	It's easy to prevent such gossip; it's a breeze!
	The contract can be drawn in secret if you please.
Arnolphe	*(still talking to himself)*:
	How should I deal with her? Oh, if I could have known . . .

Notary:	Just take her dowry and add it to your own.
Arnolphe	*(still unaware)*:
	I love her. It's this love that troubles all my senses.
Notary:	Then set a larger sum for her own expenses.
Arnolphe	*(continuing to talk to himself)*:
	But how should I treat her in such a circumstance?
Notary:	The husband has to give to the wife in advance
	One third of her dowry; but that's just official,
	You can give her much more, not to be superficial.
Arnolphe	*(still talking to himself)*:
	If . . . *(he notices the notary)*
Notary:	A "preference share" is also just as good.
	A husband can provide for his wife's widowhood
	As soon as he decides.
Arnolphe	*(at last fully aware of the notary's presence)*: Huh?
Notary:	If he loves his wife,

A man should endeavor to protect her for life
By jointure or perhaps some other settlement
That can be made invalid in the sad event
Of her demise; unless it will go to her heirs
Either through the law regarding these affairs
Or as a "deed of gift" by the contract's provision
Of "mutual consent" or "private decision".
Why shrug your shoulders so? Do you think I've no clue
How to draw a contract? Is that what worries you?
Then who might teach me this? No one, to save my life!
Do you think I don't know that a husband and wife
Share by common law all goods and property
Unless one gives the other formal authority
Over his or her part? Don't I know that one third

Of her dowry goes . . .

Arnolphe: Oh, please don't be absurd.

I'm sure you know all that; who asked you to explain?

Notary: You! . . . who'd like to make me look stupid or insane

Grimacing at me while I'm talking to you.

Arnolphe: May this man go to hell; his ugly dog face too!

Farewell: this is the way to make you disappear.

Notary: Isn't it for the contract that you've called me here?

Arnolphe: Yes, I did send for you, but now things are delayed.

I'll call you when the time is right, don't be afraid.

What nonsense from this man; he's evil, I suspect.

Notary *(alone)*: I think something's hit him; my thinking is correct.

Scene III

The Notary, Alain, Georgette

Notary   *(going towards Alain and Georgette who've just entered)*:

Have you come to fetch me for your master again?

Alain: Yes.

Notary: You might know better what kind of specimen

He is. I have a message you can give him though:

Tell him he's a blockhead.

Georgette: We'll certainly do so.

Scene IV

Alain, Georgette, Arnolphe

Alain   *(as Arnolphe enters)*:

              Master . . .

Arnolphe: Please come closer. You are my faithful friends.

              I have some news on which my own future depends.

Alain: The Notary has said . . .

Arnolphe: Leave him. It's been delayed.

              My honor was at stake when that shrewd trick was played.

              It would have been an insult to you, I dare say,

              To see your master lose his honor in this way.

              You would not be able in public to appear,

              Everyone, seeing you, would point at you and sneer.

              Since this is your business as much as it is mine,

              You have to be adept and try to undermine

              That young gallant's efforts, so he has no way to . . .

Georgette: You've taught us our lesson, we know just what to do.

Arnolphe: Don't let his charming words make you forget yourselves.

Alain: Oh, please! . . .

Georgette: We do know how to defend ourselves.

Arnolphe: If he whispers softly: "Alain, my poor heart

              Needs your help and comfort so it won't break apart."

Alain: You are a fool.

Arnolphe: That's good. "Oh, my little Georgette,

              You are the kindest person in the world, I bet!"

Georgette: You are a booby!

Arnolphe: Good. "But what harm can you find

              In the honest intent of a virtuous mind?"

Alain: You are a rogue.

Arnolphe: That's great. "Oh, my death is sure

              If you show no pity at the pain I endure."

Alain: You are a . . . shameless fool.

Arnolphe: That's very good! "You see,

I'm not one to expect any favors for free,

And those who serve me well know that I don't forget.

Here, Alain, get yourself a drink. And you, Georgette,

Go buy a petticoat to change your attitude;

(giving them money which they eagerly take)

And this is just a token of my gratitude.

I'd ask you for nothing, yet I cannot suppress

My only wish: to see your beautiful mistress."

Georgette: Tell that to someone else!

Arnolphe: Good one.

Alain: Get out!

Arnolphe: Good.

Georgette: *(pushing Arnolphe):*   Now!

Arnolphe: Good. Hey! that's quite enough.

Georgette: Did I do wrong somehow?

Alain: Isn't this what you meant by us being "adept"?

Arnolphe: Yes, except for the cash which you shouldn't have kept.

Georgette: Oh, no! I am afraid we really missed that part.

Alain: Perhaps you'd like us to review it from the start.

Arnolphe: No, enough! Go inside.

Alain: You just have to say so.

Arnolphe: No, I tell you! Go in. I order you to go!

Keep the money. Now leave! I will join you later.

Mind my words and watch out for that instigator.

Scene V

Arnolphe   *(alone):* I will ask the cobbler who has a precise eye

And lives right on this street to be my private spy.

I'll keep her in the house all day long, starting now,

And have her guarded well. Then, I shall not allow

Any hair dressers, ribbon or wig vendors,

Makers of handkerchiefs, gloves and other "splendors",

All those who employ these underhanded fashions

To encourage love's enigmatic passions.

I, too, have been around; I know their craftiness.

My man should be endowed with more than cleverness

To get a love letter or message past my guard.

Scene VI

Horace, Arnolphe

Horace: I'm glad to find you here. Thank God, I'm still unscarred

For that was a close call, a quite narrow escape.

When I left you, I was surprised to see the shape

Of the lovely Agnes in that balcony there

Next to those tall trees, enjoying the fresh air.

After she signaled me, then she did even more:

She came down to the garden and opened the door.

But we've hardly succeeded in getting to her room

When she heard coming up her jealous future "groom",

And all that she could do in this situation

Was: lock me in the closet without hesitation.

He came in right away. I saw nothing, but heard

Him stride around the room without saying a word,

Letting out now and then a few pitiful sighs,

Punching the furniture from what I could surmise,

Kicking a little dog who made a sorry sound

And throwing on the ground all the clothes that he found.

Then, with a hateful hand he smashed a vase or more

Which decked the fireplace of the one I adore.

I thought this horned cuckold must know something, no doubt,

About the tricks she played; but how did he find out?

So after several moments of pure doom,

His anger evenly discharged around the room,

My jealous worrier, not stating his complaint,

Left the room. I came out, feeling a little faint.

We both agreed to part for the gentleman had

Inspired fear in us, as he seemed quite mad.

It was too much to risk if we were to be found.

I'll slip into her room tonight without a sound;

I must cough three times to let her know I'm here,

She'll open the window as soon as she'll hear.

Then, I'll climb a ladder, gazing at her sweet face,

And love will carry me to her tender embrace.

I've told you this because our friendship is unique.

My heart's delight augments with every word I speak.

No matter how great a man's happiness may be,

It's never perfect if no one else knows but he.

I think you'll want to know whether I did succeed.

Good-bye. I'm going to prepare what I need.

Scene VII

Arnolphe   *(alone)*:

So this obstinate fate that brings me to despair

Will not give me the time to take a breath of air?

My prudent vigilance receives blow after blow,

Confounded by their wit. It enrages me so,

That in my ripe, old age I have become the fool

Of that innocent girl barely out of school,

And her scatterbrained beau. For twenty years I,

A sage philosopher, have watched husbands comply

With their sad fates. I've studied all the accidents

That push the most prudent into bad incidents.

I've profited a lot from others' disgraced life

And I've searched many ways, after picking a wife,

To guard myself against attacks of any kind

And be different from those who seem utterly blind.

I wanted to apply towards this noble goal

All cleverness and skill of the human soul.

It's as if fate itself has issued a decree

That no husband can be exempt from cuckoldry.

After all the knowledge and the experience

I've gained on these matters through work and common sense,

After twenty years or more of meditation,

Taking all precautions into consideration,

Have I tried to be different from husbands that I've seen

Only to find myself exactly where they've been?

Cursed fate, you want to trick me, but you won't succeed

For I still have in hand the object of his need.

If that distressing fop has now stolen her heart,

At least I'll make sure he'll steal no other part;

And this night that they've picked for such a gallant feat

Will not be, as they think, neither smooth nor too sweet.

It gives me satisfaction, despite my sad mishap,

To be so well informed of my awaiting trap,

For that heedless young fool who wants to harm me so

Has placed his confidence in his rival and foe.

Scene VIII

Chrysalde, Arnolphe

Chrysalde:	Well, my friend, shall we dine before we take a walk?
Arnolphe:	No, I'm fasting tonight.
Chrysalde:	What's with this whim? Please talk.
Arnolphe:	Excuse me, please. I've got some troubles, I admit.
Chrysalde:	The wedding you have planned will still take place, won't it?
Arnolphe:	You're too concerned about the lives of other men.
Chrysalde:	My, such a sudden change! What is your sorrow, then?

Could it be that you've had some problems, my old friend,

And the smooth course of love has now come to an end?

I'd swear that's it. Your face reflects just what I said.

Arnolphe: Whatever may happen, at least I'm still ahead

Of certain characters who will calmly admit

Those gallants to their homes, for their wives' benefit.

Chrysalde: It's very strange that you, being this enlightened

About all these matters, should yet be so frightened

And base upon such things your supreme happiness

As if there's just one way to honor and success.

Being stingy, brutal, a coward or a cheat

Doesn't mean much to you compared to this feat.

A man may have lived well, he may be good and bold,

But he's honorable only if he's not a cuckold.

Why do you want to base our glory and good name

On simple accidents for which we're not to blame?

And why should one reproach his own sensible soul

For a misfortune which is beyond his control?

Thus should a man be praised or blamed because he chose

A wife who misbehaves under his very nose?

And why must he create out of her faithlessness

Such a frightful monster to prove his helplessness?

If one's a gentleman, one should be able to

Deal with cuckoldry easier than you do.

Since no one is exempt from the blows of chance,

One should be indifferent in such a circumstance.

After all, misfortune is only as bad as

One chooses to see it, and so, if a man has

The wisdom to avoid any kind of excess,

Then he will surpass all hardships with success.

One shouldn't imitate those men who are so meek

As to even take pride in the way that they speak

Of what goes on between their wives and those gallants

Whom they praise everywhere, extolling their talents.

Some even form a bond with their wife's Chevalier,

Accepting all his gifts, attending each soirée

Without any scruples; and thus, society

Is right to be so shocked at their impiety.

This behavior's wrong without a doubt, I know,

But the other extreme can be even more so.

If I don't like those wives who have lovers galore,

I also disapprove of men who rage and roar,

And whose impudent wail like a storm unfurled

Attracts through its loud noise the eyes of the whole world

As if they wouldn't want anyone to ignore

Any of the causes that have made them so sore.

Between these two extremes there is a middle way

From which the prudent man should never ever stray;

And if he takes this road, he will never turn red

At the worst shame his wife can bring upon his head.

In short, there is no need to look at cuckoldry

As at a frightening and cruel misery.

As I've told you before, the trick is just to make

The best of everything, even your worst mistake.

Arnolphe: After this great lecture, the whole fraternity

Owes thanks to your Lordship for such integrity.

You should attract new members to join your lovely group:

Cuckolds Inc., or better: The Married Nincompoop.

Chrysalde: Hey, that's not what I meant. I condemn such things too.

But since fate is the one who gives a wife to you,

You should treat this the same as a game of dice where

If you don't get what you want, you take care

To use your skill and reduce your licentiousness,

Changing your luck through patience and judiciousness.

Arnolphe: So I should just eat, sleep well, and try to flatter

Myself that what goes on doesn't even matter.

Chrysalde: You're making fun of this, but, to be sincere,

In the world there are other things you should fear;

Things which are more likely to cause you endless pain

Than this small incident which scares you in vain.

And if I were given two choices in your stead,

I would prefer to be exactly what you said

Rather than be wed to one of those flawless wives

Whose bad temper can make a trial of men's lives.

Those dragons of virtue, those devils in disguise

Hide behind their morals and like to patronize

Everyone around them on the strength of one wrong

They've never committed. And we must go along

With all the miseries they bring into our lives

On the account that they've always been faithful wives.

Once more, my dear pal, learn for your benefit

That cuckoldry is only what you make of it

For in some instances one might welcome this state

And, as with everything, make the most of his fate.

Arnolphe: If you want to resign yourself to make the best

Of this state, go ahead. I'm not willing to test

This on me. I swear that I will never be . . .

Chrysalde: By God, don't swear please; you'll commit perjury!

If this is what fate wants, it is useless to fight.

No one cares about what you may think is right.

Arnolphe: Then I'll be a cuckold?

Chrysalde: Come on, it's not so bad.

Other people are too, and they have never had

Your character, your heart, your fine education

And much less your great financial situation.

Arnolphe: And they'll never have it! I'm beyond compare.

But your jesting words are more than I can bear.

That's enough, if you please.

Chrysalde: You're angry, I can tell.

I wonder why . . . Good-bye, and remember this well:

Whatever your honor inspires you to do,

When you've sworn that something will not happen to you,

That *something*'s half accomplished even while you swear.

Arnolphe   *(alone)*:

             I'll swear it again. I just need to prepare

             Some means of protection against such an event.

             (he runs to knock at his own door)

Scene IX

Arnolphe, Alain, Georgette

Arnolphe   *(to Alain and Georgette who have opened the door)*:

             My friends, I'm begging you for help. I am content

             To feel your affection, but now I have to see

             How, in this occasion, you will prove it to me.

             If you respect my trust and serve me well, you'll be

             Properly rewarded, that's a certainty.

             The man you know so well—and keep your mouths shut

             tight—

             Wants, as I have found out, to deceive me tonight.

             He'll enter Agnes' room by scaling the wall.

             We'll ambush him. We are three people after all.

             I want you each to have in your hands a good stick

             And when he's reached the ladder's top, you must be quick

             (The window will be open, I'll take care of it)

             And attack this traitor. However you must hit

             Him hard enough to leave a souvenir or two

             On his back so he'll learn that this house is taboo.

             And don't mention my name whatever else you do

             Nor let him guess that I'm directly behind you.

             Well, are you capable to serve my anger thus?

Alain: When it comes to hitting, leave everything to us.

	You'll see that when I hit, I have a deadly hand.
Georgette:	Mine only seems weaker, but not many can stand
	Its blows. I am quite strong and hardly ever miss.
~~Alain:~~ Arnolphe	Then, go in. Remember: not a word about this!
	(alone):
	This is a useful lesson to be handed down,
	And if all the husbands who inhabit this town
	Would greet their wives' gallants with my wisdom and strength,
	The list of cuckolds' names would be reduced in length.

ACT V

Scene I

Arnolphe, Alain, Georgette

Arnolphe:	Traitors, what have you done? Why all this violence?
Alain:	It was only to prove our obedience.
Arnolphe:	This excuse is useless, it won't work at all.
	My order was to hit not kill, if you recall,
	And it was on the back rather than the head
	Where you should have landed your best blows, like I said.
	Heavens! This accident of fate fills me with dread
	For how will I bear to see that young man dead?
	Go back inside the house and do not say a word
	About some innocent order you may have heard.
	(alone):
	It's dawn. I must think how to behave in the face
	Of such a misfortune, what to do in this case.
	What will become of me? What will his father say
	When he'll suddenly learn of what happened today?

Scene II

Horace, Arnolphe

Horace	*(aside)*:
	I should see who this is to set my mind at ease.
Arnolphe	*(thinking he is alone)*:
	Who could have predicted?

(noticing Horace but not recognizing him):

          Who is there, please?

Horace: Sir Arnolphe?

Arnolphe: Yes. But you? . . .

Horace: It's Horace. I was just

On my way to ask you for a favor. You must

Get up pretty early!

Arnolphe   *(aside, softly)*: I'm in such confusion!

Is this a magic spell or some strange illusion?

Horace: I was in deep trouble, as a matter of fact,

But now I thank Heaven for its generous act

That made me find you here exactly when I needed.

I'd like to tell you that everything's succeeded

Much better than I hoped, and through an incident

Meant to destroy it all. I mean, it's evident

That someone has found out about our rendezvous,

But how this was discovered, I don't have a clue.

I was close to reaching the window of my love

When I saw two people appearing above

Who, suddenly lifting their arms without a sound,

Made me miss the last step, so I fell to the ground.

This fall left some bruises that make me mildly sore,

But at least it saved me from twenty blows or more.

I think my jealous friend was among them as well.

They all thought their clubbing was the reason I fell,

And since the pain made me stay still for quite some time,

They believed they'd killed me, and afraid of the crime

They had just committed, they accused each other.

Oh, I could hear them fighting one another.

In the nightly silence so intense and profound,

Their shouts and accusations made a frightful sound.

Then, without a candle and still fighting, they came

To see if I was dead. I kept playing their game

And, acting as a corpse, cloaked by the deep dark night,

I gave those two bastards quite a terrible fright.

They retreated quickly as if under a spell.

And as I was thinking of retreating as well,

I saw my sweet Agnes hurrying towards me.

My feigned death was for her a real tragedy.

Those fools' words had reached her and filled her with emotion,

So she took advantage of all the commotion

And being less observed, she managed easily

To escape from the house and run out secretly.

When she found me alive, pure joy replaced her grief.

Her genuine delight was beyond my belief.

What can I say? This girl, this lovable sweet dove

Has followed the advice dictated by her love.

She refused to go back to that tyrant's commands

And so she placed her fate in my worshipping hands.

Just think of how that madman's vain impertinence

Has exposed her innate unspoiled innocence

To great perils which might have damaged her virtue

If I didn't adore her as much as I do.

But my soul is captured by a love so pure

I'd rather die than cheat her. It's her sweet allure

That makes her worthy of a better fate. I vow

That nothing except death can separate us now.

I can anticipate a paternal fit,

But we'll attempt to calm my father bit by bit.

Her gentle, lovely charms have swept me off my feet.

In life one should fulfill one's dreams to feel complete.

I'd like to ask of you to let me put my sweet,

Charming girl in your hands; but you must be discreet.

Please do me this favor; take my Agnes with you

And hide her in your home just for a day or two.

Her escape must be kept secret to the world's eyes.

People might start a search and even send out spies.

Any girl of her age being seen with a man

Might arouse suspicions. Now I know that I can

Trust you to be cautious. Since I have given you

My total confidence as you've always been true

And generous to me, also to you alone

Can I entrust the one whose heart I'm proud to own.

Arnolphe: I am at your service; never doubt that, my boy.

Horace: You'd do me this favor which would bring me such joy?

Arnolphe: Of course, it's my pleasure. I'm simply delighted

And the chance to serve you gets me so excited

That I must thank Heaven for giving me this chore.

I've never been so glad to help someone before!

Horace: I'm so indebted to your generosity.

I feared you would make difficulties for me.

But since you are so wise, a true man of the world,

You can understand youth and its passions unfurled.

My man's at the corner, keeping her in his sight.

Arnolphe: But how will we proceed? For it's almost daylight.

If I meet her here perhaps someone will see.

If she's brought to my house, there will certainly be

Talk among the servants. I think, to be more sure,

You should bring her to me in a place more obscure;

	That dark alley seems safe; I'll wait for her right there.
Horace:	Such precautions are wise in this kind of affair.
	I'll leave her in your hands, and then I must return
	Quietly to my place, not to arouse concern.
Arnolphe	*(alone)*:
	Fortune! This stroke of luck is one of your best gifts.
	It repairs the evil of your capricious shifts.
	(he covers his face with his cloak)

Scene III

Agnes, Horace, Arnolphe

Horace	*(to Agnes)*:
	The place where I will take you is safe, you can be sure.
	Don't worry. You will be protected and secure.
	You cannot stay with me: remember what I said.
	You must go through this gate, and let yourself be led.
	(Arnolphe takes Agnes by the hand without her recognizing him)
Agnes	*(to Horace)*:
	Why are you leaving me?
Horace:	Oh, dear Agnes, I must.
Agnes:	But you'll come back to me very soon, I trust . . .
Horace:	Trust my amorous flame to bring me to you fast.
Agnes:	Ah, when I don't see you, my misery is vast.
Horace:	When I'm away from you, I feel sad too, my dear.
Agnes:	Oh, no! If that were so, you'd stay with me right here.
Horace:	How can you doubt my love that's so ardent and true?
Agnes:	No, you do not love me as much as I love you.
	(Arnolphe pulls her hand):

I'm being pulled too hard.

Horace: Well, we're in danger here.

What if someone sees us together, Agnes dear?

This splendid friend of mine who is pulling your hand

Is watching out for us. Please, you must understand.

Agnes: I don't even know him . . .

Horace: Don't be afraid, my love.

In his trustworthy hands you'll be safe, my sweet dove.

Agnes: It's in Horace's hands where I'd prefer to stay.

Horace: And I'd . . .

Agnes: *(to Arnolphe, who is pulling her):*

                   Wait . . .

Horace: The daylight is chasing me away.

Agnes: When will I see you then?

Horace: Very soon, certainly.

Agnes: Until that moment comes, I'll suffer horribly!

Horace   *(leaving):*

Now I can sleep. Thank God for His few miracles

That saved my happiness from future obstacles.

Scene IV

Arnolphe   *(covering his face and disguising his voice):*

Come with me. Don't worry, I won't have you stay there.

You'll hide in a refuge I've prepared elsewhere;

I can only put you in the best, safest place.

(uncovering himself):

Do you recognize me?

Agnes: Ah!

Arnolphe: You cheating minx! My face

Certainly frightens you in this moment of truth.

You hate seeing me here and rebel in your youth

Because I'm in the way of your hot love affair.

(Agnes looks around for Horace)

Don't look for him; there's nothing all around but air.

He's already too far to help you anyway.

Aha! You are so young and yet . . . the tricks you play! . . .

So, in your innocence which seemed unequaled here,

You once asked me if children are born through the ear.

Yes, you! . . . who can set up a nightly rendezvous

And flee the house in secret, your lover to pursue.

I'll be damned! How your mouth can run on with that fool!

One would say you'd been taught in an excellent school.

Where the hell did you learn so much so soon, Agnes?

And aren't you afraid of spirits in the darkness?

This nightly visitor has made you bold I see.

Vixen! I can't believe your wicked perfidy!

You reward my kindness by doing me this wrong!

Oh, viper that I've nursed at my breast for so long,

You have grown up only to try to harm the one

Who has cared for you as no one's ever done!

Agnes:	Why do you shout at me?
Arnolphe:	Oh, so I'm wrong, somehow!
Agnes:	I don't see any harm in all I've done 'till now.
Arnolphe:	Following a gallant is not an evil act?
Agnes:	He wants me for his wife; we made a sacred pact.
	I've learned your lessons well; you've always preached to me
	That one must wed to avoid sin and infamy.
Arnolphe:	Yes; but you were to be my wife as I had planned.
	I made it clear enough for you to understand.

Agnes: You did. But, between us, I tell you honestly:

He is more to my taste than you will ever be.

You say that marriage is so troublesome and grim,

So dull and tiresome; it's not that way with him.

Oh, he makes it sound like a haven of pleasure.

Now my wish to marry really knows no measure.

Arnolphe: Ah! You love him, traitress!

Agnes: Yes, I love him. I do!

Arnolphe: And you're telling me this? By God, how dare you?

Agnes: Why shouldn't I tell you if it's true? I'm sincere.

Arnolphe: But should you have loved him, you vixen?

Agnes: Oh, dear!

What else could I have done? He made me. I must say

I wasn't planning to; it just happened this way.

Arnolphe: You should have chased away that amorous desire.

Agnes: How can I chase away what sets my soul on fire?

Arnolphe: Didn't you stop to think that I might be offended?

Agnes: No, not at all. But why? There was no harm intended.

Arnolphe: Great! Now I can rejoice. Thank you for your noblesse.

In that case, does this mean you don't love me?

Agnes: You?

Arnolphe: Yes.

Agnes: Oh, dear! No.

Arnolphe: What? No?

Agnes: Do you want me to lie?

Arnolphe: Tell me, Miss Impudence, why don't you love me? Why?

Agnes: By God, it's not my fault that you couldn't be

Or try to make yourself as lovable as he.

I don't think I've stopped you from doing that, have I?

Arnolphe: I have gone to such lengths. Oh, I really did try,

	But my hardest efforts were just uselessly spent.
Agnes:	He just knows more than you, I think that's evident.
	Well, he made me love him with no effort at all.
Arnolphe	*(aside)*:
	The vixen! She reasons and answers with such gall.
	Damn! Those coquettes couldn't have done better than she.
	Either I misjudged her or, by God, can it be
	That this young fool knows more than the cleverest man?
	(to Agnes):
	Since reason is consuming your mind, perhaps you can
	Tell me, sweet logician, through your reasoning sense:
	Is it for him I've raised you so long at my expense?
Agnes:	He'll pay back everything, not a single crown less.
Arnolphe	*(aside, softly)*:
	She has a way with words that doubles my distress.
	(loud):
	But will he pay me back everything else you owe?
	All your obligations to me? I don't think so.
Agnes:	I doubt my obligations are really that great.
Arnolphe:	Raising you from childhood means nothing, you ingrate?
Agnes:	Oh, you've done that so well! What an inspiration
	To bestow on me this lovely education!
	Do you think I'm flattered? Do you think I can't see
	That I'm just like a beast, ignorant as can be?
	I am ashamed myself above all, at my age.
	Being seen as a fool fills me with bitter rage.
Arnolphe:	Then, to flee ignorance, you try to take a course
	In wisdom from that fop, that gallant fool . . .
Agnes:	Of course.
	From him I have learned things I never knew before.

| | You may think I owe you, but I owe him much more. |

Arnolphe: I don't know what restrains me from smacking her face
For these insolent words that increase my disgrace.
I fume at her coldness, it's tearing me apart;
Punching her a few times would satisfy my heart.

Agnes: Oh, dear! Go ahead, if that's how you'll be pleased

Arnolphe *(aside)*:

By those words and glances my anger is appeased.
I can feel the rebirth of tenderness in me
Erasing her foul deeds and evil treachery.
What a strange thing is love! Due to these traitresses
Men become subject to a thousand weaknesses!
Everyone knows their faults and their love of deceit;
They are extravagant and always indiscreet.
They have a frail soul and quite an evil mind,
There's nothing sillier or weaker than their kind,
And nothing more faithless. But despite all of this,
One can do anything for these animals' bliss.

(to Agnes):

Well now, little traitress, let's make peace. And what's more,
I forgive all you've done and love you as before.
Reflect upon this act which shows my love for you,
And return my kindness by loving me too.

Agnes: I would like to please you with my whole heart and soul.
But what would it cost me to accomplish this goal?

Arnolphe: My poor dear, if you wish you can please me for free.

(he sighs)

Just listen to that sigh, as loving as can be.
Observe my whole being and my languishing glance,
And leave that snotty boy and his foolish romance.

He must have put a spell on you and your young life.

You'll be a hundred times happier as my wife.

You have a passion for merriment and finesse;

I swear you'll have it all as you wish, no less.

Day and night I'll caress you, kiss you, eat you up,

Snuggle and cuddle you, you'll be my butter-cup.

You can do what you wish; I'll let you have your way.

I won't explain myself, that's all I have to say.

(aside):

How passion can drive me to frightening extremes!

(loud):

My love cannot be equaled even in your dreams.

Ungrateful girl! Tell me what kind of proof you need.

You want to see me cry? Beat myself 'till I bleed?

You want me to pull out my hairs one by one?

Or should I kill myself? If you want it, it's done!

Cruel girl, I'm ready to prove my love's sincere.

Agnes: Listen, all your speeches don't touch my soul, that's clear.

With a couple of words Horace could do much more.

Arnolphe: Ah! You've pushed me too far, and this I can't ignore.

I will follow my plan, you indocile blockhead,

And away from this town you will soon be led.

You reject all my vows and you drive me insane,

A convent cell will be the revenge for my pain.

Scene V

Alain, Agnes, Arnolphe

Alain: I don't know if it's true or I'm under the weather,

	But Agnes and that corpse have just left together.
Arnolphe:	She's with me. Go put her in my room, the last place
	He'd try to look for her. Well, in any case,
	It's just for half an hour, not a minute more,
	'Till I find a carriage and bring it to my door
	To take her where it's safer. Now, you and Georgette
	Keep your eyes on her. And lock up, don't forget.
	(alone):
	I'm thinking if her soul changes its location,
	It might soon be rid of this infatuation.

Scene VI

Arnolphe, Horace

Horace:	Ah! I've come to find you. I'm overwhelmed with pain.
	Heaven has made my plight even more inhumane
	Through its cruel, unjust, fatal plot from above
	To tear me away from the beauty I love.
	My father had decided to arrive today.
	Well, I have just met him; he's not too far away.
	The reason for his visit was a mystery
	And now it's been revealed: he has married me
	Without letting me know, and wants to celebrate
	The marriage he's arranged. You can appreciate
	The awful state I'm in. The whole thing is absurd;
	It is the worst disaster that could have occurred.
	This Enrique about whom I asked you yesterday
	Has caused the misfortune that weighs me down today.
	He's arrived with my father to ruin my life:

It's his only daughter that will become my wife.

Oh, I thought I would faint hearing what they said.

When my father told me he'd call on you, I fled

As quickly as I could, I wanted to get here

Before he did. My mind is paralyzed with fear.

I beg you, don't reveal anything that you know

About my engagement, it could anger him so.

And since he really trusts you, please try to dissuade

My father from the match which he has just made.

Arnolphe: Yes, indeed.

Horace: Advise him to postpone things a bit.

My friend, do this for love and for my benefit.

Arnolphe: I shall not fail you!

Horace: I put my hopes in you.

Arnolphe: Great!

Horace: You're the truest father that I ever knew!

Tell him that at my age . . . He's coming, I can see.

Here are some arguments you can use to help me.

(Horace pulls Arnolphe to a corner of the stage to talk to him secretly)

Scene VII

Enrique, Oronte, Chrysalde, Horace, Arnolphe

Enrique *(to Chrysalde)*:

As soon as I laid eyes on you, my dear Sir,

If you hadn't told me, I'd have known who you were.

You look like your sister who was so kind and sweet;

Being married to her made my life complete.

I'd be so happy if the harsh Fates had let me

Take this devoted wife to see her family

And enjoy the sweetness that a return home brings,

Especially after our long sufferings.

But since we're deprived of her dear presence for good

Through the fatal power of destiny, we should

Try to resign ourselves, and be pleased with the last

Existing evidence of our love and our past.

This concerns you deeply, and without your consent

I would be very wrong to pursue my intent.

No doubt, Oronte's son is an excellent choice,

But it should please you too so we can both rejoice.

Chrysalde: You don't respect my judgment to doubt that I'll agree

With the choice that's been made. It seems rightful to me.

Arnolphe *(aside, to Horace)*:

Yes, I want to help you the best way I know how.

Horace *(aside, to Arnolphe)*:

Once more, keep my secret . . .

Arnolphe *(to Horace)*:

Of course. Don't worry now.

(Arnolphe leaves Horace to join the others and embrace Oronte)

Oronte *(to Arnolphe)*:

Ah! What a warm embrace filled with such tenderness!

Arnolphe: Seeing you makes me burst with sheer happiness!

Oronte: Well, I have come here . . .

Arnolphe: No need to say a word.

I know what has brought you.

Oronte: You have already heard?

Arnolphe: Yes.

Oronte: Great!

Arnolphe: Your son resists the marriage planned for him

And his prejudiced heart sees it as sad and grim.

He has even begged me to make you change your mind.

But I advise you that, if you should be inclined

To delay this marriage, you'd make a big mistake;

You'd put your paternal authority at stake.

All young people should be kept under strict control.

If we are indulgent, we can damage their soul.

Horace   *(aside)*: Traitor!

Chrysalde: If this choice seems repulsive to his heart,

Then we shouldn't force him. That wouldn't be too smart.

And I think my brother will agree with me.

Arnolphe: He'd let his son govern him to such a degree?

Do you want a father to be so weak and mild

As not to demand obedience from his child?

It would be a fine thing, subject for ridicule,

If we were to be ruled by the ones we should rule!

No, no; he's my close friend and his honor is mine.

He has given his word, now he shouldn't decline.

So let him show how firm he is, and make his son

Abandon forever his former liaison.

Oronte: He's right. As for this match, I will now guarantee

My son's obedience and docility.

Chrysalde   *(to Arnolphe)*:

I am greatly surprised to see your eagerness

About this engagement, and I can hardly guess

The mysterious cause that makes you act this way.

Arnolphe: I know what I am doing and say what I must say.

Oronte: Yes, of course, Sir Arnolphe . . .

Chrysalde: That name makes him sore.

	Call him Sir de Stump as I've told you before.
Arnolphe:	No matter . . .
Horace	*(aside)*: What is this?
Arnolphe	*(turning to Horace)*: The mystery, my son.
	Now you see the reason for everything I've done.
Horace	*(aside)*:
	I'm perplexed . . .

Scene VIII

Georgette, Enrique, Oronte, Chrysalde, Horace, Arnolphe

Georgette:	Sir, please come! For without you around,
	We can't hold Agnes back, and we can tell she's bound
	To escape anytime. Maybe she'll even throw
	Herself out the window. She might do it, you know.
Arnolphe:	You might as well bring her to me since I intend
	To take her away. Don't be angry, my friend,
	For too much happiness can go to a man's head.
	Each man gets his own turn, as the proverb has said.
Horace	*(aside)*:
	Oh, Heavens! What misfortunes can equal my own?
	What man's seen the abyss into which I've been thrown?
Arnolphe:	You'd better hurry up and set the marriage date.
	I'll be glad to attend. Oh, I can hardly wait!
Oronte:	That is my intention.

Scene IX

Agnes, Alain, Georgette, Oronte, Enrique, Arnolphe, Horace, Chrysalde

Arnolphe	*(to Agnes)*:	Come, my beauty, come here.

So, you're hard to hold back and quite wild, I hear.

Here is your sweetheart. Go on, reward the man.

Drop him a nice curtsy as humbly as you can.

(to Horace):

Good-bye. You are a bit disappointed, it seems.

Oh, well. Not all lovers get to fulfill their dreams.

Agnes: Horace, will you let him take me away from you?

Horace: Ah! My pain is so strong, I don't know what to do.

Arnolphe: Let's go now, chatterbox.

Agnes: But I want to stay here.

Oronte: Explain this mystery, we're all dying to hear.

We just can't understand what this is all about.

Arnolphe: When I'll have more time, I'll tell you all, no doubt.

Good-bye.

Oronte: Where are you going? I didn't expect

You to behave this way and show us no respect.

Arnolphe: But I did advise you to ignore your son

And finish the wedding.

Oronte: Yes. But to get it done,

Since you've learned everything, don't you know that the bride

Is living in the very place where you reside?

The daughter that was born to the sweet Angelique

From her secret marriage to Seigneur Enrique?

So what was all that talk based on? Explain yourself.

Chrysalde: I must admit I am quite astonished myself.

Arnolphe:	What? . . .
Chrysalde:	My dear sister had a daughter secretly
	Whose fate was kept hidden from the whole family.
Oronte:	Her husband took the girl to the country where she
	Was raised under fake names, to keep the secrecy.
Chrysalde:	Then fate turned against him and dealt him a bad hand,
	So he was forced to leave his dear native land . . .
Oronte:	And brave thousands of perils far beyond the sea,
	In those distant places unknown to you or me.
Chrysalde:	And there, through hard work, he managed to complete
	The fortune he'd lost here to envy and deceit.
Oronte:	As soon as he returned to France, he couldn't wait
	And sought the woman he'd charged with his daughter's fate.
Chrysalde:	And the peasant woman told him frankly that she
	Had given the small girl to you in custody.
Oronte:	She had been forced to call upon your charity
	Since she was overwhelmed by extreme poverty.
Chrysalde:	And he, filled with delight, happiness and good cheer,
	Has taken the old woman and has brought her here.
Oronte:	She will be arriving to clear the mystery
	In front of everyone, as you soon shall see.
Chrysalde	*(to Arnolphe)*:
	I can guess your anguish and your predicament,
	But fate doesn't favor you in this incident.
	If not being a cuckold means so much to you,
	Then don't marry at all, that's the best thing to do.
Arnolphe	*(leaving, too overwhelmed to speak)*:
	Oh!
Oronte:	He's left without a word. Why?
Horace:	Ah! Father dear,

This mystery will be uncovered, have no fear.

It seems to me that Fortune might have read your mind

When she carried out here the wise plan you'd designed.

I'd given my word to this beauty, no other,

A mutual love bound us to one another.

But she's also the girl you came to find; the one

Whose hand I rejected as an ungrateful son.

Enrique: The moment I saw her, that is just what I thought.

My soul was deeply moved for I found what I'd sought.

Ah! My daughter, I yield to transports of delight.

Chrysalde: Brother, I'd do the same, but this isn't quite

The proper place for that. I think we should all go

Inside and put in order everything we know.

Then we must thank our friend for his help in our quest,

And Providence which does everything for the best.

4594245R00055

Printed in Great Britain
by Amazon.co.uk, Ltd.,
Marston Gate.